Christmas, 2015

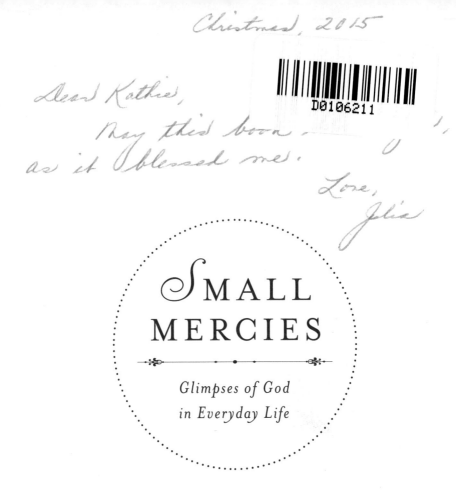

Dear Kathie,

May this book . . . . ,
as it blessed me.

Love,
Jlia

SMALL MERCIES

Glimpses of God in Everyday Life

NANCY JO SULLIVAN

LOYOLAPRESS.
A JESUIT MINISTRY
Chicago

LOYOLA PRESS.
A JESUIT MINISTRY

3441 N. Ashland Avenue
Chicago, Illinois 60657
(800) 621-1008
www.loyolapress.com

Art credit: iStockphotography.com

Library of Congress Cataloging-in-Publication Data
Sullivan, Nancy Jo, 1956-
  Small mercies : glimpses of God in everyday life / Nancy Jo Sullivan.
    p. cm.
  ISBN-13: 978-0-8294-3695-2
  ISBN-10: 0-8294-3695-2
1. Spirituality. 2. Sullivan, Nancy Jo, 1956- I. Title.
  BV4501.3.S855 2012
  248--dc23

                                                                2011050525

Printed in the United States of America
12 13 14 15 16 17 Bang 10 9 8 7 6 5 4 3 2 1

For Christina, Rachael, and Sarah

Contents

Small Mercies

I live near the Cathedral of Saint Paul. The grand edifice sits on a hill that overlooks the downtown area of Saint Paul. Built in the early 1900s and inspired by French Renaissance architecture, the outside walls are made from rock granite that was dug from Minnesota quarries. Crowning this historical landmark is a copper-covered dome that can be seen for miles.

In my memories, the Cathedral will always hold a special place. On rainy days, when my three daughters were very young, I would load them in our van and drive to the hillside sanctuary to spend an hour or two. It was a way of breaking up the monotony of a day when we couldn't go to the park or play in the backyard.

Under gilded ceilings and glass-lined chandeliers, the girls and I would stroll through the empty church, passing statues of saints that were twenty times bigger than we were. As the rain pattered over the dome, we would study the scripture stories that were illuminated on mosaics of colored glass. While the organist practiced in the balcony, we would light votive candles, one for each of us.

Most of the time, the girls could keep themselves occupied while I took a few moments to sit quietly and relish the peace and quiet. Within those 100-year-old walls, their little voices never rose to more than a whisper.

Sometimes they would point to the ceiling and try to guess how many angels were painted on the inside dome. Other times, they would visit the chapels in the back of the church and take turns signing themselves with holy water. One afternoon, my two youngest daughters, Rachael and T.T. sat next to me in a pew reading a Bible that we had brought along. But out of the corner of my eye, I noticed Sarah, then about 9, walking down the middle aisle with slow measured steps. She pretended to hold a bouquet of flowers. "Mom, I . . . I . . . feel like a bride . . . " she stuttered softly. She passed by, all the while sprinkling make-believe petals over the aisle. I turned to her and whispered: "You are . . . "

Those afternoons at the Cathedral always made me feel as if heaven was just within my reach. Here, there were no clothes to fold, no house to clean, no errands to run. Underneath this copper dome, the kids were well behaved and God's presence could be easily seen, heard, and felt. His mercies seemed to be everywhere.

All these years later, I'm transitioning from full-time motherhood into a brand new stage of life. Even so, the girls and I still like going to the Cathedral for holiday masses or Confirmations. But on rainy afternoons, just as in days gone by, I often slip away to the Cathedral to relish a few moments of stillness.

To me, this space will always feel like heaven. My faith is anchored in the signs, symbols, and stories that surround me. Yet, I know something now that I didn't know as a young mother.

God's presence cannot be contained, even in this master-piece of a church.

The years have taught me that the Lord's presence is easily accessed in the places and faces that define our daily lives. Indeed, the most precious revelations of God's love are often hidden in the ordinary moments that shape our days. I call these revelations small mercies.

We can find God's small mercies in the mundane conversations we share at the kitchen table or in the unexpected chats we have with strangers. When we encourage a coworker, support a friend, or receive the care of a loved one, God's mercies shine brightly, like votive candles. In laughter that doubles us over or in heartaches we think we will never survive, the small mercies of God cover us, like rain pattering over a dome.

Each time we experience a small mercy: a hopeful word, a compassionate hug, or promise of forgiveness, we are called to remember that we are loved by a God who is immeasurably bigger than we are. Though he is a glorious God, worthy of the most splendid residence, he lives and moves among us, making his home in our heart.

My name is Nancy Jo Sullivan. In the coming chapters, I will be sharing some of the ways in which I've caught a glimpse of God in my own life. In sharing these reflections, I will be praying that you will be on the lookout for the Lord's presence in your own life.

I will also be inviting you to take a new look at the timeworn practices of prayer, fasting, and almsgiving. Yes, I know that these disciplines are centuries old, but they are the lens through which we can magnify the tiniest revelations of God's love.

As you turn these pages, it is my hope that you will begin to notice the petals of small mercies that God has sprinkled over your life.

They're everywhere.

1

The Divine Touch

One winter, now twenty-six years ago, it got so cold that ice formed inside the kitchen windowpanes. Gasoline froze in the tank of our family car. Bare, brittle limbs snapped in the breeze, and newscasters warned of windchill and frostbite. Despite the bitter weather, I walked alone each morning through our new neighborhood, dressed in layers of down and wool.

I walked and I walked. Maybe defying the elements made me feel I had some control over my life. That year, I had lost two loved ones to death, and our first baby had been born with Down's syndrome. As much as I loved our child Sarah, I still felt stunned. God seemed concealed, hidden somewhere in this cold winter of death and disappointment. So I trudged in solitude, day after freezing day. Only in front of a stranger's brick house did I become gradually aware of a presence, a kind of peace. Here, for a moment each morning, I felt something promising, hopeful, and reassuring. I didn't know why.

Spring finally did come, and children once again pedaled bicycles on the sidewalk, men swung golf clubs on the green fairways, and I exchanged my down and wool layers for jerseys and faded blue jeans.

One morning, I took Sarah in her stroller along with me on my walk. In the bright sunlight in front of the brick house, I saw a mother playing with her young twin daughters. I watched as she gently guided the girls' hands over rough bark and offered them lilac blooms to smell. Just when I realized that the children were blind, the mother greeted me with a wave.

"May they touch your baby?" she asked. While the two girls softly stroked Sarah's face, brushed her fine hair, and held her tiny hands, their mother spoke about what it had been like when her children were born and what unexpected blessings she had found in those early years. "In adversity, we must be alert," she said, "for God will find a way, somehow, to touch us."

I wondered whether I should tell her about my walks. Finally, I said, "Last winter I passed by your home each morning. I felt strangely reassured and comforted. Warmed."

My new friend smiled. "You must be the person I felt compelled to pray for this winter. I thought someone in this neighborhood was going through a difficult time. Now I know it was you."

Now that I am older and wiser, I often think back on my journey of mothering a special child. Sarah's life, though difficult, held many moments of grace. One of the most memorable took place on that spring day in my neighbor's front yard. I didn't know it then, but as the little girls touched the face of my baby, they were giving me a tender image of God, one that would sustain me for years.

Throughout Sarah's brief stay on earth, I felt the divine touch of God. Even on days when she struggled with speech, reading, daily cares, hearing loss, impaired vision, and—in the last years—a terminal illness, I heard God whisper, "I am closer than you think."

God *was* close. Every burden of Sarah's disability was balanced by the sweetness of her spirit and the fullness of her unconditional love. Whenever she smiled, I caught a glimpse of heaven. I often thought, *Someone must be praying for me.*

These days, when I see a young mom with a special-needs child, I want to hold out my arms to her. I want to proclaim the words of St. Elizabeth when she met Mary on that long-ago day in Palestine: "Blessed are you among women, and blessed is the fruit of your womb" (Luke 1:42). But I always restrain myself. I don't want to intrude on her life. Instead, I pray for her, just as my neighbor once prayed for me. In God's own time and with God's own methods, I know that this mother will also feel the divine touch.

God is always closer than we think. He will never leave or forsake his children. In times of uncertainty, we must remain alert; God will find a way, somehow, to touch us.

Receive the Mercies

Prayer
Pay attention to the small promptings that tell you to pray for someone. These little nudges are small mercies that come from God's heart.

Fasting
Fast from an unalert life. Take notice of the ways in which God is making himself known to you.

Almsgiving
Offer prayer for a stranger. Your intercession will bless him or her in ways you will never know.

Adapted and reprinted with permission from Guideposts. Copyright 1996 by Guideposts. All rights reserved.

2

Empty Nest

Three years ago, on a hot August morning, I moved my youngest daughter into her college dorm. She was the last of my daughters to leave home. "Mom, I'm on my own now; you have to let me go," Rachael said as we unloaded boxes filled with pillows and sheets. "I'll be fine," I told her, trying to be stoic.

Now it was 9:00 in the evening. I flopped onto the couch in our living room. I could hear the sound of a clock ticking in the hallway, the hum of the air-conditioner, and a slow drip from the kitchen faucet.

What I didn't hear were the familiar sounds that had filled the walls for years: the boisterous voices of my three daughters, the whir of hair dryers, the ringing of phones, the loud blasts of music, and the constant footsteps going up and down the stairs.

I'm an empty nester, I thought. I bristled at the phrase. It brought to mind images of a lonely old mother, a used-up parent without a purpose.

But without children at home to care for, "empty nester" seemed like the only title left for me. For years, I had defined myself almost exclusively as a mother. Although I had always worked outside the home, my family had been the center of my universe, and the needs of my daughters shaped my daily routines. I made meals, did the laundry, baked birthday cakes, and sewed Halloween costumes. I drove the kids to sports events, the dentist, and dance practices. I read stories, rehearsed lines for plays, and helped with homework. I shopped for prom dresses, curled long locks of hair, and hosted graduation parties. Being a mother was my vocation. Caretaking was a familiar and comfortable lifestyle for me.

I know that every mom goes through some sort of empty-nest transition, but mine had an extra wrinkle. In addition to saying a wrenching good-bye to my two college-bound daughters, I was still saying good-bye to my oldest daughter, Sarah, who had died only a year before. She was the one daughter I had expected to be with me in my older years, because her disability kept her dependent on me. Even while my other daughters were growing into responsible young adults, Sarah had remained childlike in some ways. I had grown used to caring for her special needs and rejoicing in her humble achievements. She often joked with me by saying, "Mom, I will take care of you when you are in a wheelchair."

But it seemed that no one needed me anymore. Many of my friends who had college-aged children were putting their homes up for sale and moving into smaller houses or town-homes. I couldn't imagine leaving my house—it held too many good memories.

The fall and winter months passed quickly. My job kept me busy during the day, but every night the empty house seemed to swallow me up.

Then, one spring afternoon, on my way home from work, I stopped by a small hillside church that overlooked the Catholic college I had attended when I was young. The sign above the entryway still read "Our Lady of Victory Chapel."

I knelt in a pew, glad that no one was around. The sunlight streamed in through the stained-glass windows, and the chapel felt quiet and still. As a young coed I had often visited this chapel to think, pray, and dream. Here, long before becoming a mother, I had begun imagining my future: *I'll get married, raise a family, write a book, and travel to Ireland.* I'd also envisioned my ideal home: a small cottage surrounded by wildflowers, a picket fence, and a screened-in porch with wicker furniture.

Now, so many years later, it was clear that my life hadn't turned out quite the way I thought it would. I had given birth to a child with disabilities. I had divorced in my forties. For several years I had known the stresses and strains of being a single mom. I had lost a child.

I couldn't believe I was in my fifties. I'd been so busy caretaking and surviving the losses of my life that I'd forgotten how to dream.

I glanced at the altar. There, etched in the stone table were six words that had endured the decades: "Behold, I make all things new . . ."

In that sacred silence, God whispered, "I'm restoring you." But what did that mean exactly?

Just a few days later, my next-door neighbor had a garage sale. Between card tables brimming with glassware and trinkets, I found two wicker chairs priced at twenty dollars each. They were antiques, covered with layers of peeling paint, but they were still sturdy. I thought they would look great in my cottage-to-be.

Something amazing was happening. For the first time in years, I wasn't thinking about who needed my attention. I was dreaming about my future—*my* future.

I bought the chairs. Carrying them through my backyard, I giggled a little. This was so exciting! I imagined how the chairs would look after I painted them. I decided to make new cushions for them.

Since that day at the garage sale, I've come to appreciate, not loathe, this new and exciting stage of life. I will always treasure the years I spent mothering my kids, and I cannot erase the losses I have survived. But I have said yes to the new thing God is doing.

Now I'm writing the books I've longed to write for years. My sisters and I are planning a trip to Ireland. Most important, I've surrounded myself with friends, like-minded people who refuse to live a dreamless life.

My two-story home still feels big, but I'm saving up for that little cottage with the picket fence—it's just a matter of time before I find it. When I do, I'll pack up my memories, and with God's help, I'll take them all with me.

As for the wicker chairs, they're in the basement right next to the laundry room, freshly painted. I call them my hope chairs. Each day, on my way to do the wash, I look at them and feel hope and anticipation.

The repurposed chairs have become a powerful metaphor, not only for me, but for all women who are embarking on the second half of life. In the post-children era, we are called to renewal and recreation. Our lives are full of promise and possibilities. In Christ, we are so much more than empty nesters. We are followers of dreams, receivers of hope, and women of victory.

Our days of raising kids may be over, but behold! God has made all things new.

Receive the Mercies

Prayer
Pray that God might give you the courage to follow your dreams. Don't let your age keep you from pursuing the vision God has given you.

Fasting
Fast from the belief that your life has no purpose or meaning. Let the small mercies of new dreams move you forward.

Almsgiving
Offer the alms of your life experience to a young parent. Your wisdom is a small mercy that you are called to share.

3

Scrapbooks

I sat at the kitchen table, sifting through years of family photos that had been stored in plastic boxes. Now that my daughters were in their early twenties, it was time to organize their childhood memories into scrapbooks.

As I spread the pictures out on the table, I began sorting them into categories: baby pictures, preschool programs, junior high dances, sports events, graduations, and proms.

It was a good day to stay indoors. The cold January winds blew outside the kitchen window. A few days earlier, I had bought ten scrapbooks on sale, each one with a different colored cover. My goal for today was to fill these empty pages with images of life as it once was.

Soon the past was laid out on the table like a carpet. *How did time go by so fast?* I lifted an old family photo into my hands, one that was taken when I was a young mom. In the picture, I had big hair and wore a fuchsia dress with shoulder pads. Rachael, then just a baby, sat on my lap, her pudgy fingers clasped together. Six-year-old Sarah rested her hand on my shoulder. She wore pink-framed glasses, and her freckled face bore an angelic radiance. T.T., our precocious three-year-old, smiled broadly. All three girls wore matching dresses of flowered cotton that I had sewn. Centered in the middle of us all was Don, the husband of my youth. Looking young and dapper, he wore a suit and tie.

So much had changed. Now that I was in my fifties, my days no longer revolved around the nonstop routines of caring for my family. Rachael was away at college, studying for a medical career. T.T. was a first-year social worker who served families of people with disabilities. Both of them were intelligent, quick-witted, and kind. They had grown into responsible young women who were beautiful inside and out. They still dropped by the house at least once a week to visit. I often said to them, "I'm so proud of you."

But our family's blessings had been counterbalanced with heartaches, our loss of Sarah the most profound and recent. Her terminal illness and death had been like a tsunami, a giant wave of grief that had slammed over our lives. Although time had healed the worst of our wounds, we were still picking up the debris of our sadness.

And there was the loss of a marriage. It's hard to say how much Sarah's mental and physical challenges contributed to the fracturing of Don's and my relationship. Perhaps the stress of caring for a child with disabilities distracted us from the erosion that was taking place in our marriage. The marriage had failed, but we would always be bonded through the indissolvable love we had for our daughters. Our experience of raising them could not be erased from our collective memory.

As the snow began falling outside, my eyes moved to and fro over the collage of photos that covered the table. I pressed on with my project, tucking a batch of first communion and confirmation photos into a scrapbook with a white cover.

Lost in thought, I began thinking about how the experiences of divorce and death had altered our family. For a moment, I let myself feel the pain of all that had been lost, yet I could not discount the myriad healings that had come. During the months following Sarah's death, Don and I had made our peace. The two of us had come to realize that we could build a friendship rooted in the experiences we had shared as a family. Although we could not fix our relationship, we agreed that we could give each other the next best thing: acceptance.

I looked out the window and watched the snow drifting into our driveway. I tried to remember how many years it had been since the divorce. Ten?

Lately, some of my friends had been encouraging me to start dating. "It's time," they said. But the thought of going out to dinner or sharing a walk with someone was almost overwhelming. It seemed awkward to think about having someone new in my life. It would take courage to see myself as someone other than a wife or mother. But after so many years of taking care of my family, I could at least think about the possibility of a new relationship. *Does God want that for me?*

I opened a red-covered scrapbook and began filling it with pictures from Thanksgivings and Christmases. There was part of me that wanted to stay safely huddled in the past, like the photos I was sealing into the book. *If I met someone I liked, what would I have to offer?*

For the rest of the afternoon, I filled the scrapbooks with snapshots of days I would always cherish: family vacations at the lake, picnics at the zoo, and graduation parties in our backyard.

Later that night, after finishing all ten memory books, I filed them on a shelf in the family room, glad that the task was done.

Having been cooped up all day, I decided to take a walk outside. It had stopped snowing, and the winds had calmed down. Bundled in a down jacket and warm gloves, I stepped outside my house and breathed in the crisp winter air. I walked through the freshly fallen snow, the stars twinkling above me.

I began having a quiet dialogue with God. *I could never give someone my past. That belongs to Don, the kids, and me.*

In the silence, I could feel God's loving presence reaching out to me. My past was a treasury of stories, some painful to recall and others beautiful to behold. My family history would be a part of me forever. *Yes, Lord, I've learned so much.*

But God wasn't finished with the story. Tomorrow was waiting to be lived. In the days ahead, God would journey with me, just as he had in the past. There might even be room for a new relationship.

I looked upward. The soft starlight felt comforting. I put out my hands as if waiting to receive something. *I give you the future,* I said.

That was an empty scrapbook waiting to be filled.

Receive the Mercies

Prayer

Pray over this passage: "For surely I know the plans I have for you, says the Lord, plans for your welfare and not for harm, to give you a future with hope" (Jeremiah 29:11).

Fasting

Fast from the urge to live in your past. Remember that it's possible to cherish the past without setting up camp there.

Almsgiving

Allow God to give you the alms of courage. This is a small mercy that will move you forward.

4

New Drapes

After my divorce, ten years ago, I isolated myself from my family. Although I needed their support more than ever, I avoided their ongoing offers to chat on the phone or to go out for coffee. I didn't want to face their questions: What happened? Did you try to work things out? Why didn't you tell us sooner?

I had grown up in a clan of committed Irish Catholics. Divorce had never been a big part of our history. My parents had been married for thirty-five years and had stayed together until the day my father died. My siblings, all eight of them, were happily married and bringing up their children. My aunts and uncles were celebrating their golden wedding anniversaries.

Attending family gatherings was like being on stage in front of a live audience. *This is awkward*, I thought, while conversing at family picnics and parties. I was doing my best to pretend that nothing had changed. But really, I wanted to curl up and hide. How could I tell anyone how scared I was to be on my own?

When I went to Mass, I felt out of place there, too. I was a single mom worshipping in a sea of married couples. Somehow life seemed less sacred now that I was single. Did God still love me?

As I tried to adjust to the single life, I poured myself into caring for my three teenage daughters. I was glad for the distraction. My girls needed me, especially Sarah. I kept myself busy with house projects: cleaning out gutters, organizing closets, and patching up the driveway.

Then, one Saturday morning, I was painting the living room, when my sisters, Peggy and Julie, knocked on the front door. Both in their early forties, they stood on my step in jeans and T-shirts. "Lattes anyone?" Peggy feigned a French accent and held three cups of coffee she'd bought from a nearby shop.

"We brought breakfast." Julie held up a white bag filled with chocolate doughnuts.

I motioned for them to come inside, feeling conspicuous in my paint-splattered, oversize sweatshirt. "The house is a mess . . . The girls are still asleep."

We walked around the tarp-covered furniture. The smell of fresh paint filled the room. We sat down on the floor, next to the ladder, and Peggy handed me one of the coffees. "I love the wall color," she said.

"The room looks so much bigger," said Julie, munching on a doughnut.

"It's called Morning Sunshine," I said.

While we talked about paint chips and wall textures, neither of them mentioned the invisible elephant in the room that was tromping around us: my divorce. They seemed to sense, as sisters so often do, that I wasn't ready to delve into all the details.

Peggy grabbed a home-decorating catalog from a nearby footstool. "Are you going to buy new curtains?"

"Yeah. I was thinking about the taupe-colored drapes on page 36." I pointed to a picture of an expensive pair of silk curtains. "I really can't afford them right now."

Peggy kept paging through the catalog. "There's a discount fabric store by my house. Let's run over there. We could probably find the same drapery fabric at half the price."

Peggy and her family lived in an upscale suburb about a half hour away. Although her house was near a wealthy gated community, she had chosen to decorate her home on a shoestring budget. A skilled seamstress, she had sewn most of her home decor—bedspreads, table runners, and drapes. Her house was a soothing refuge filled with stripes, checks, and florals. She had also upholstered many pieces in her home—one-of-a-kind finds that she had single-handedly brought to life from various sales.

Julie picked up a tape measure and began measuring my windows. "We need about eighteen yards of fabric."

Awhile later, the three of us arrived at the fabric store. Women on a mission, we rummaged through the bolts of fabric that had been marked down to three dollars a yard. Peggy pulled out a roll of taupe silk, the same color as the drapes we had seen in the catalog. She waved the fabric above her head like a flag.

But that roll held barely a yard of material. "Not enough," I said, feeling skeptical about this whole enterprise.

Julie kept digging, her head hardly visible above the piled remnants. "We can't give up." After a moment, she plucked another bolt of silk from the table. "It's taupe!" Julie reminded me of a referee calling a touchdown. We gave each other high fives.

As I rummaged through the discounted material, I suddenly spied three bolts that were neatly stacked underneath the table. I motioned my sisters to draw near. "Taupe!" we called out in unison.

Our fabric-filled cart wobbled and squeaked as we wheeled it to the cash register. "That will be thirty-seven dollars and twenty-three cents," said the clerk. Peggy handed her two twenty-dollar bills. "These are on me."

A few days later, Peggy and Julie came over with a portable sewing machine. While Peggy sat at my kitchen table, sewing the discounted silk into drapes, I hung new curtain rods in my living room. Meanwhile, Julie ironed each panel, one by one.

Late in the afternoon, after the final drape had been hung, the three of us stood back and admired our work. "Move over, Pottery Barn," Julie announced.

I looked at my sisters. "I don't know what to say . . ."

My life was a mess. Yet they hadn't asked for explanations, sought answers, or passed judgment. Instead, they had come bearing coffee, doughnuts, and hand-sewn curtains. Theirs was the gift of unconditional acceptance. They had brought beauty to my home and, in doing so, a little healing to my heart.

At one time or another, every person goes through difficulty. During such times, we need not isolate ourselves from those who love us most. God has placed them in our life for a reason. Even when it feels awkward to be cared for, we should let it happen. Those who love us are the ones who will find a way to ease our pain and give us hope.

Through them, Christ can love us—even when we tell ourselves that we are doing just fine.

Receive the Mercies

Prayer
Pray that you might receive, with open arms, the support of loved ones. Let them offer you the small mercies of comfort, acceptance, and laughter.

Fasting
Fast from the temptation to isolate yourself from those who love you. Your friends and family will be there for you even when your life is a mess.

Almsgiving
Give the alms of a treat to a friend. Healing often begins with something as simple as a cup of coffee.

5

A Dog Named Sabbath

An orange sunrise cast a glow over the houses in my neighborhood. It was early spring, but a few patches of snow lingered from the long winter. On that quiet Sunday morning, I jogged past a yard framed with a chain-link fence. Lost in thought, I hardly noticed the black dog that paced behind it.

As a single woman in my early fifties, I was going through a major life transition. Over the previous two decades, I had invested my time and energy in bringing up three daughters and keeping up my house. Now that the girls were in their early twenties, away at college and living their own lives, I was just beginning to explore the question, Who am I now?

My life was not void of meaning. As the director of several ministries at a vibrant church, I found great fulfillment in the programs I coordinated and the people I served. I had a good network of friends and family. New writing projects were coming my way.

But that morning, worrisome questions raced through my mind. *What does the future hold? Will I be able to make ends meet? Will I grow old alone?*

Then I heard the dog growl. In the dawning sun, his eyes looked like two pieces of coal, his open mouth revealing sharp teeth that made me think of icicles hanging from a roof.

I'm glad there's a fence.

Slinking back and forth, the dog eyed me through the chain links. He kept pace with each step I took. I watched as he lumbered up a snow bank that hadn't yet melted. Atop the white mound, he stood upright, his front paws on top of the fence.

"Don't jump . . ." I prayed softly.

Too late. The dog flung mightily into the air. He leaped over the fence like a plane taking off from a runway. For a few seconds, he was suspended between the ground and sky. I closed my eyes. I could hear a guttural growl and the sound of his paws hitting the street and galloping toward me. "This is it," I said.

Then everything slowed down. I opened my eyes, planted my feet, and held one hand up in front of me like a police officer directing traffic. "Stop!" I hardly recognized my voice—the tone was low, and it sounded powerful, even authoritative.

The dog came to a complete halt. "I'm in control," I told the dog. He cocked his head to the left and looked at me as if confused.

I stared him down, feeling something like Luke Skywalker in the old *Star Wars* movies, my outstretched hand a light saber.

A few seconds later, the dog's owner came rushing out the back door of his house and saw me holding the dog at bay. The man's weathered face revealed his age, and although I wanted to reprimand him for not watching his dog more closely, I just stood there, relishing the thought that I had actually stopped a beast. "Sabbath! Get over here right now," he said.

On command, the dog named Sabbath leaped back into his yard.

As I jogged onward that morning, the sun warmed my face. Though still a little shaken, I knew that Sabbath had shown me something important about myself.

My fears about the future had growled at me long enough. Now it was clear that God had given me a voice to stop my worries in their tracks. "The Lord will provide everything I need," I said with newfound resolve.

We all must face worries about the future, but God has given us the power to halt our fears in their tracks. We don't need to be timid or tremble uncontrollably. When Jesus was in the desert he confronted the devil with boldness. Jesus' words, spoken with authority, caused the powers of darkness to flee.

When we lift our voices in prayer, we are equipped to battle every doom-filled thought. In the Scriptures we read: "Do not worry about anything, but in everything by prayer and supplication with thanksgiving let your requests be made known to God. And the peace of God, which surpasses all understanding, will guard your hearts and your minds in Christ Jesus" (Philippians 4:6–7).

The next time the beast of your anxiety leaps out at you, don't close your eyes and wait for the attack. Stand firm in Christ. Fold your hands in prayer. Feel God's power and shout, "Stop!" You might discover a voice you never knew you had.

Receive the Mercies

Prayer
When you feel anxiety, imagine the Lord shielding you on all sides. Ask him to guard you from all worry. Receive the small mercies of his comfort and peace.

Fasting
Fast from fretting. Instead, dream a new dream.

Almsgiving
Give the alms of encouragement to a worrisome friend.

6

The Twitch of Hope

As I've already mentioned, my daughter Sarah was born with Down's syndrome. Everything about her was bright and shiny. Her eyes twinkled. Her smile was like a beam of sunshine. Her laughter could warm the coldest soul. Although she lived only twenty-three years and could not function mentally beyond the level of a second-grader, she taught us many lessons of faith, hope, and love. She was the center of her mother's heart.

Then, on one of the coldest days of winter, she passed away. In the months that followed her death, people would ask, "How are you doing?" I never knew how to answer that question because the experience of losing my child was impossible to explain.

But now that a few years have passed, a story from Sarah's infancy keeps surfacing in my memory. Each time I remember it, I am better able to understand and clarify what I have learned from grief.

When Sarah was just nine months old, she was recovering from open-heart surgery in a sterile intensive care unit. As first-time parents, Don and I took turns keeping a round-the-clock vigil at her stainless-steel crib. For weeks, our daily schedules revolved around visits to the hospital. Don stayed with Sarah at night, and I took the day shift.

At six each morning, I found myself gearing up for another difficult day beside Sarah's crib. The fluorescent ceiling lights made me want to put on sunglasses. In contrast, the darkness of despair wrapped around me like a thick fog. As the nurses changed Sarah's bandages, I wanted to intervene and rescue her. *She's just a baby.* While the doctors adjusted her breathing tube, a monitor recorded each beat of her heart. I longed to cradle Sarah in my arms, but there was no guarantee that she would even survive.

What was hardest for me was seeing my baby lying lifeless, twenty-four hours a day. As part of her postoperative treatment, the doctors had given her the drug Pavulon to temporarily paralyze her muscles. They explained that it was an "essential medication," one that would allow her body to recover at a slow pace from the trauma of surgery. "The stillness will bring healing to her heart," one doctor said.

Day after day, her eyes never opened. She couldn't move her arms or legs. Her stillness was profound. As I traced the sign of the cross on her forehead, I wondered if she could hear my voice. "I'll never leave you," I said.

The weeks dragged on and on. I was worn and tired. It seemed that my tiny daughter would never recover.

Then one morning, a nurse named Marion drew near. Gray haired and sporting a Mickey Mouse scrub top, she reminded me of my grandmother. "Your baby is making progress." Her smile was comforting.

I held Sarah's tiny hand. "Progress?" I asked. As far as I could tell, nothing about Sarah's condition had changed in weeks.

"The doctors said we can take out her breathing tube. You should be able to hold her in your arms this afternoon."

"Really?" Could it be true? Was Sarah going to wake up?

The nurse nodded, her eyes filled with compassion. "Really."

Over the following few hours, I watched as Marion carefully weaned Sarah from all the machines and tubes that had been sustaining her life.

"Watch for small movements in her muscles. It will happen very slowly."

For hours, I sat nervously at Sarah's bedside. It was her fingertips that began to twitch first, like little sparks igniting. I put my hand over my mouth and wondered whether my eyes were deceiving me. "She's moving," I told the nurse. The little toes wiggled, and my eyes misted.

"It won't be much longer," said Marion.

I leaned in, waiting for my baby to open her eyes. Sarah began to stretch out her arms as if she was waking up from a long nap. I gently touched her eyelids. "Take your time, Sarah. There's no hurry," I said.

She blinked a couple of times. Several minutes passed. I waited. I watched. Then, it happened. Slowly, she opened her eyes. For a moment, she gazed at me as if she was studying my face. Our glances were locked.

"I forgot your eyes were green," I told her.

With tenderness, Marion wrapped Sarah in a blanket and placed her in my arms. "I'll let you two get reacquainted."

I rocked her in my arms. I couldn't take my eyes off her. "Sarah, you have a brand-new life."

On that long-ago day in intensive care, Sarah began living a wonderful life that lasted more than two decades. From her first years on earth until her very last day, she brought goodness and mercy to our lives.

When she died, I am certain that the angels welcomed her with open arms. But as her mother, I could not bring myself to celebrate my child's heavenly homegoing. During the cold winter weeks that followed her death, I was completely paralyzed. I stopped working at my job. I slept away the frigid days and nights. Most of the time, my eyes were shut. "I don't want to recover," I told myself.

The winter dragged on. Crippled by grief, I lay lifeless in my own personal intensive-care unit. But there, in that dimly lit place where faith is tried and unspeakable sorrow is faced, I met God.

God did not appear before me in all his power and glory. I couldn't see his face. Instead, God came to me in the profound stillness. As all the routines of my life came to an abrupt halt, he never left my side. Each day, he worked in silence, repairing my heart. As I slept, he touched my eyelids and whispered, "I'll never leave you."

When the snow and ice finally began melting around my house, I got up one morning and made my way to our backyard. It had been months since I had gone outside without a winter jacket. Near the deck, one green shoot was poking through a patch of soil, a sprout from a day lily.

I lifted my eyes toward the blue and sunlit sky and felt a warm breeze blow through my hair. Something felt different. I was awake, moving and standing in my garden. *Take your time, there's no hurry*, said an inner voice.

I took a deep breath of fresh air. "I've survived," I said. I felt a tiny twitch of hope.

Since that spring morning, the twitch of hope keeps rousing me from my grief. I'm back at work. I'm writing again. I'm enjoying the love and support of family and friends. I've even started to pursue some dreams that have been dormant since my youth.

I'm still in the process of mourning Sarah's loss. I'm sure that I will grieve her absence for many years to come. Even so, I feel as if I have gotten up from a long nap. Although my heart will always bear the scar of her death, I am moving. I am stretching my arms out to hope. I am living a brand-new life.

Today, if you find yourself grieving the loss of a loved one, be at peace. Let yourself rest in the intensive care unit of your soul. Stay there as long as you need to. Don't rush the healing. In the stillness, you will find God. In the silence of your unspeakable sorrow, he will slowly mend your heart.

But remember, someday soon, when you least expect it, the twitch of hope will come.

Receive the Mercies

Prayer

Pray that you will begin to recognize the twitch of hope in your own life. Hope is a small mercy that brings great healing.

Fasting

Fast from trying to heal your heart. Only God can do that. In times of grief, remember: "The LORD is near to the broken-hearted and saves the crushed in spirit" (Psalm 34:18).

Almsgiving

Give a friend the alms of your comfort and stay with him or her in stillness.

7

Jesus at the Door

I've never felt unsafe in my home. My next-door neighbor—I'll call him Broad-Shouldered Bob—is the sheriff of a nearby county. He watches over our streets like a lion protecting his pride. Tom, a family physician, lives just a few houses away. He's married to my longtime friend Mary. All my neighbors have large dogs.

When friends knock on my door, they see a welcome wreath and a security sticker proclaiming that my home is protected. Sometimes it seems that my safety depends on people, pets, and alarms. But whenever I start thinking this way, thoughts of my sister Annie come to mind.

From the time Annie was a baby, I watched over her like a second mother. I was only five when she was born, but I often fed her a bottle, rocked her to sleep, and took her for rides in a stroller. We were inseparable.

During her teenage years, my little sister transformed into a head-turning beauty. She had white teeth and long legs and wavy hair like Farah Fawcett's. She was lovely to behold, but her wild spirit was uncontainable. She partied hard, much to my parent's dismay. She smoked cigarettes, and some of her friends were troublemakers. Sometimes she would call me late at night and ask me to pick her up from a crowded party. "Annie, you've got to take better care of yourself," I would tell her. I was the nagging older sister.

In her early twenties, Annie moved into her first place, a one-room apartment on the third floor of a dilapidated old house. At the time she worked as a hotel receptionist and barely had enough money to live on. "Nancy, my new place is so cool," she told me one night on the phone. "I got a great deal on rent."

"I can't wait to see it. I'll come on Saturday."

When I first pulled into the driveway of Annie's rental, I double-checked the address she had given me.

"Oh, no!" The house looked like something out of a late-night horror show. The shutters were falling off, and some of the windows were cracked. There was no railing in the stairway that led to her third-floor space. I was glad I had worn sweats and tennis shoes; I might as well have been hiking up a mountain path. On my way up, I passed the window of another apartment and saw that it was draped with an American flag. A long-haired guy with a ponytail peeled away the flag and waved to me. He looked like someone I had seen in pictures of Woodstock. I could hear the sound of an electric guitar and smell cigarettes.

"Annie!" I knocked on a rickety old door. In the round space where a doorknob should've been was a wooden insert. I rolled my eyes.

"Hey, sis! Let me give you a tour." Annie motioned for me to come inside. She wore an oversized sweatshirt and a base-ball cap.

"Wow, this is really something," I said, trying to sound impressed. Her entire apartment was no bigger than the bedroom we had shared as kids.

The two of us stood in the center of the room, where the roof came to a point. It was the only place where we could both stand upright. A toaster oven and a small fridge were tucked under an open cabinet that held a box of Lucky Charms and three cans of Dr. Pepper. Her bed was a twin mattress squeezed into an alcove beneath a cracked window.

"Do you like my statues?" she asked, pointing to a small shelf that held haloed figures of Mary, Joseph, and St. Francis. Next to her front door stood a waist-high statue of Jesus carved from heavy stone. His arms were outstretched. I jumped when I saw him.

"It's nice that they fit so well in here," I said. As we sat down on her mattress, Annie handed me a can of Dr. Pepper. I told myself to remain positive. A few months earlier, Annie had had a religious conversion while attending a Catholic Charismatic Renewal conference. She had stopped smoking and had left behind her partying ways. Her social circle had completely changed, and she was hanging around with friends who shared her newfound faith. As Annie put it, she was "living for the Lord."

I could hear rock music playing in the apartment below.

"Well, at least you know you're protected," I said, glancing toward the statue of Jesus.

As I drove home from her house, I couldn't help but wonder whether Annie's spiritual transformation was starting to impede her common sense. God wouldn't stop a break-in if her front door didn't have a lock.

A few days later, early in the morning, I dropped by her apartment to check on her. I had stopped at a hardware store and picked up a deadbolt lock for her door. After climbing the summit of the stairs, I began knocking on her front door.

"Annie? Are you up?" I put my ear to the door and listened. No answer.

I started to get worried. My mind started racing with dreadful thoughts. *Someone has broken in, and that guy downstairs has kidnapped her.* I leaned into the door, using all my weight to try and open it. It budged, but only an inch or two. Something heavy was behind it. I wiggled my hand into a small gap and felt something stony. It was an outstretched hand.

I gasped. "It's Jesus!" I was holding onto the statue.

A few seconds later, I heard Annie moving the stone figure away from her entryway. "Geez, this thing is heavy," she said.

When the door was open, I looked at her sternly. "Annie, a statue won't keep you safe."

My sister shrugged and smiled. She seemed completely unfazed. "Hey—would you break into a house if Jesus was guarding the door?"

Decades have passed since that day at Annie's little apartment. She's happily married now, a committed Christian and a conscientious mother who is homeschooling her daughter. I'm proud of who she has become.

But so many years ago, Annie imparted an important life lesson that remains with me even as I move into my older years. By placing her total trust in God, she taught me that deadbolts, even the best ones, can never offer true protection. Only God can do that.

In Psalm 139:7–10 we read: "Where can I go from your spirit? Or where can I flee from your presence? If I ascend to heaven, you are there; if I make my bed in Sheol, you are there. If I take the wings of the morning and settle at the farthest limits of the sea, even there your hand shall lead me, and your right hand shall hold me fast."

God is our ultimate security system. Unlike an alarm that can lose its power or a dog that can be distracted, the Lord keeps a constant vigil over our lives.

I suppose, though, if I had a moment when I felt unsafe in my home, I wouldn't hesitate to put a statue of Jesus in my entryway. After all, who would break in if Jesus was guarding the door?

Receive the Mercies

Prayer
Visualize Jesus standing at your front door. Imagine him with outstretched arms, tenderly blessing you and your loved ones. Receive the small mercies of his presence and protection.

Fasting
Fast from the fear that you will be harmed. Meditate on these words from verse 2 of Psalm 144: "[The Lord] is my rock and my fortress, my stronghold and my deliverer, my shield, in whom I take refuge, who subdues the peoples under me."

Almsgiving
Give the alms of reassurance to someone who feels unprotected. Be the presence of Christ in that person's life.

8

Date Cookies

When my family gets together for Thanksgiving, we often sit around a large table and reminisce about the past. As we eat turkey and pie, my grown siblings and I—all eight of us—try to outdo one another in passing along our funniest remembrances to our young nieces and nephews.

"Tell the date cookie story," the kids will request. Though I've told the tale many times, the youngsters never tire of hearing it. You might call it a family classic.

The story took shape years ago, on a snowy afternoon in February. Bundled in mittens and earmuffs, my sister Peggy and I rushed home from school, our breaths misting in the frozen air. I was in the fourth grade, and Peggy was just one year younger. When we opened the front door to our house, the familiar aroma of just-baked cookies greeted us.

"Oh no," I whispered.

"She made them again." Peggy groaned as she unzipped her jacket.

We looked toward the kitchen. There, our grandmother "Marma," was pulling a sheet of steaming date cookies from the oven. Dressed in a Hawaiian print housedress and fur slippers, she beckoned us to draw near. "Who wants a treat?" she asked. She held out a plate of cookies that were loaded with oatmeal and dates. Silver hair framed her wrinkled face.

"The dates look like crickets!" Peggy whispered.

Marma was our paternal grandmother. When she came to visit our family, she often stayed for six months at a time. "She forgets things. Be patient with her," our parents had told us time and time again.

Marma forgot lots of things: our names, the address of our home, and where her bedroom was located. So Peggy and I could never figure out how she could remember an eighty-year-old family recipe that had never been written down. Peggy and I hated date cookies.

"Thanks," I said as Marma handed me the whole plate.

"Mmmmm," Peggy added. She feigned delight, closed her eyes, and dramatically breathed in the aroma of Marma's cookies.

With plate in tow, Peggy and I made our way down the hallway to the room we shared. For a moment, the two of us sat on our beds, studying the cookies.

"I can't . . . I can't eat another one," Peggy said. Since Marma had arrived at our home a few weeks earlier, we had eaten date cookies every afternoon.

My sister walked over to the window and flung it open. She grabbed a cookie, took aim, and whirled it into the winter air like a Frisbee.

I giggled as snowflakes whooshed into our room. "Let me try." I wound up for the pitch and threw a cookie out the window. It landed on top of the neighbor's snow-covered birdbath.

We both doubled over, trying to muffle our laughter, because Marma was still baking in the kitchen, just yards away.

That afternoon, we threw every cookie on that plate out the window. Like miniature flying saucers, the spheres ricocheted into snowbanks and pine trees. We laughed so hard we were snorting.

Later that night, just before Peggy and I fell asleep in our beds, I started to feel guilty.

"Marma has a disease. I think we committed a sin," I said.

"Just a little sin," Peggy said as she dozed off to sleep.

The following afternoon, our family attended Saturday morning confession at our Catholic parish. Sitting in the pew next to Peggy, I couldn't stop thinking about Marma. I kept fidgeting and tapping my foot. "We've sinned," I whispered to Peggy.

"Settle down," she whispered back.

Soon it was my turn to enter the confessional. As the automatic door slowly closed behind me, Peggy waved to me from her pew. "Good luck," she called out softly.

The wooden kneeler creaked beneath my feet. It was dark except for the dim silhouette of the priest on the other side of a mesh screen. I took a deep breath. "Father, I've sinned. I hate my grandmother's cookies. I threw them in the snow."

My hands were clasped tightly in prayer as I peeked through the screen. I could see the pastor's shoulders shaking as he tried to muffle his laughter. "Next time, eat the cookies," he said. "It's a sacrifice that will please God."

After receiving absolution, I was relieved that it was over. I came out of the confessional just as Peggy was going in. I nudged her and whispered, "I told him about the cookies. God forgives us."

After Peggy's turn, the two of us met at the back of the church. We quietly discussed our penance. "We gotta eat 'em," Peggy declared.

Over the next few months, Peggy and I ate date cookies every afternoon in our room. Between the chews of oatmeal and swallows of dates, we giggled. We were both in this together. It almost seemed fun.

Looking back, I'm grateful for the precious penance we shared. As sisters we learned three immutable truths that are worth passing down to the generations:

Date cookies taste awful.

Laughter minimizes sacrifice.

And God forgives sins—even little ones.

Receive the Mercies

Prayer
Even if you haven't been to confession in a while, be open to that possibility. In this sacrament, the small mercies of grace and forgiveness will bring great healing to your life.

Fasting
Fast from the guilt of failures that have already been forgiven. God has promised to remove our sins "as far as the east is from the west."

Almsgiving
Forgive someone who has hurt you.

9

Smoothies

There's a little coffee shop nestled on a corner of Main Street, about six blocks from my home. It's called the Black Sheep, the jewel of our small town. The Black Sheep is a trendy gathering place decorated in shades of lime and dusty blue. Near the entrance, a bank of windows sheds natural light over antique church pews, glass-topped tables, and overstuffed chairs. Above a stone fireplace hangs a framed painting of a black sheep.

My two grown daughters and I try to meet at the Black Sheep at least once a week. It's a great place to spend some quality family time and to catch up on our busy lives.

Not too long ago, on a hot Saturday morning, the girls and I were standing at the counter waiting to place our orders. "Mom, why don't you try something new?" said Rachael, my youngest. She was home for the summer.

"I can't stray from my trusty steamer." I was a creature of habit who rarely ordered anything but a cup of steamed milk flavored with a few sprinkles of cinnamon.

"It's hot today. How about trying a cold smoothie?" my daughter T.T. suggested. She had just finished working out at the local gym, her long dark hair pulled into a ponytail.

Rachael shook her head. "A smoothie? No way! Mom is set in her ways."

My eyes grew wide. "Are you talking about me?" Only old people were set in their ways. I was barely a candidate for an AARP card. "I'm very flexible," I said, a hint of defensiveness in my voice. I reminded my daughters about all the ways I had changed in the past few years. I had recently put together my own Facebook page. I was adept at sending them text messages on my cell phone. I had even learned how to abbreviate a few phrases like "I luv you" and "LOL."

"Mom, you hate change," my kids proclaimed in unison. They started giving me examples. "Every night you curl up on the couch and watch *House Hunters* on HGTV. You never eat anything but oatmeal and blueberries for breakfast. You exercise for exactly thirty-five minutes a day, at exactly 5:35 a.m."

An espresso machine whirred behind the counter. "What can I get you gals today?" The young barista's arms were covered with tattoos. He wore a dark T-shirt with the coffee shop's logo. He smiled pleasantly and reached for a cup, glancing at me. "Shall I start your steamer?"

I could feel my daughters waiting to see what I would do next. I looked at the blackboard where names of several specialty drinks were posted in white chalk: chai tea, painters' mocha, apple-berry blast. "Let me think for a minute," I said.

While the girls ordered their specialty lattes, I caught a glimpse of myself in the stainless steel of the espresso machine. Although there was a quiet predictability about my life, I felt

good about the many challenges I'd survived. And there was
nothing wrong with me ordering a cinnamon steamer day after
day. This little routine made me feel secure. But maybe without even knowing it, I was becoming too comfortable with
sameness.

I fast-forwarded my thoughts. Ten years from now, would I
avoid going out to breakfast with friends because I didn't want
to give up my bowl of oatmeal? Would I choose to stay home
and watch television instead of traveling to a place I'd never
been before? Would I refuse to take an afternoon yoga class
because I had already exercised in the morning?

"I'll have a strawberry-mango smoothie with whipped
cream."

The barista smiled. "Wow, she's taking a risk," he said to
my daughters.

"Mom, this is a step in the right direction," T.T. said. She
patted me on the back like a therapist who had just witnessed
a breakthrough with a patient.

The three of us sat at a table near the windows. I put my
straw in the smoothie and took a big sip as the girls leaned
in. "Wow! This is good. I can't believe I've never tried one
of these."

Ever since that day, I've been challenging myself to try new
things at the Black Sheep. It's been an adventure. I honestly
never knew that there were so many kinds of tea.

I'm also trying to make sure that my daily routines don't
prevent me from making changes that might enrich my life.
As I grow older, I don't want to be known as an obstinate old
person who is set in her ways. I'm training myself to take more

risks. When I'm in my nineties (God willing), I still want to be open to new tastes and new adventures.

More important, I don't want to become stagnant in my relationship with God. There's no excuse for spiritual inactivity, because God is always calling us to be transformed—no matter what our age. In our wisdom years, we have more time to clean out our hearts, to discard old grudges and past regrets. These are the years to embrace forgiveness and to free ourselves from the destructive power of guilt. All of these are habits that can be disrupted and changed. The wisdom years are also a wonderful time to develop a deeper prayer life. Daily conversations with God always rejuvenate and renew the spirit.

The Scriptures remind us that God will help us make these positive changes. In the Old Testament we read: "I will give you a new heart, and a new spirit I will put within you." We are never too old to be made into the image and likeness of God.

But change isn't always easy. I realized this last Saturday morning as I sat with my daughters at the Black Sheep. While drinking my cup of chai tea, T.T. and Rachael watched in awe. "I'm so proud of you," Rachael said.

T.T. asked, "Mom, do you think you will ever order a steamer again?"

I closed my eyes and sighed. I could almost smell the fragrance of a cinnamon-sprinkled steamer. "Hmm . . . Let me think for a minute . . ."

Receive the Mercies

Prayer

As you grow older, pray that you will never become set in your ways. Allow God to sprinkle the small mercy of openness over your life.

Fasting

Fast from a rigid lifestyle. Be open to new tastes and adventures. Let God create a new heart and spirit within you.

Almsgiving

Give the alms of your flexibility to loved ones. They will notice and appreciate the change.

10

Teddy Bears

On a sunlit afternoon, the lakeside path was crowded with joggers, bikers, and children on roller blades. I walked with my daughter Rachael, our strides brisk and steady. It was the Fourth of July.

"Mom, let's pick up the pace." A college athlete, Rachael worked out daily. With her face freckled from the sun, she was in great shape.

"Let's go for it," I said. I felt proud that I could keep up with her. I was still a pretty good power walker. We strode onward at a good clip, passing the grand mansions that lined the streets.

As we rounded the walkway, the sailboats near the shoreline bobbed in the waters, clinking quietly. We could smell grilled hamburgers as we passed a park where families were gathered at picnic tables. "I'm getting hungry!" I joked.

We noticed then an elderly man walking a few feet ahead of us. He wore plaid shorts and a golf shirt and walked with a slow, awkward gait.

"He's limping," Rachael said.

We slowed down. Drawing closer, we noticed that he was carrying a worn-out teddy bear.

"I used to have a bear like that when I was a little girl," said Rachael, meeting his eye. "It was my favorite."

The man smiled, wrinkles around his eyes arching like little rainbows. "I'm carrying it for my wife. She has breast cancer." A young mother with a stroller whisked by.

"That must be hard," I said.

He took a deep breath. "She was diagnosed a few months ago. I'm training for a thirty-mile walk. I want to be in good shape so I can walk for her."

His knee was bound with a gauze bandage. I could tell that each step was an effort.

"Your wife must be a pretty special person," Rachael said.

The man nodded, sun reflecting off his bifocals. "She can't be with me while I train, so I carry the bear. It reminds me of how much I love her."

A bell from a nearby trolley rang out. "We'll pray for you and your wife," I promised as a group of joggers streamed past.

"It's been nice to meet you," Rachael added.

"My pleasure." The man waved good-bye to us, smiling as he pressed on.

Later that afternoon, as we relaxed by the lake, Rachael and I couldn't stop talking about the man with the teddy bear. "I think we were supposed to meet him," said Rachael.

"Yes, I believe that." I was lying on the grass, unable to shake the image of that old man limping with the bear in his arms. I remembered a passage from 1 Corinthians 13:4–7 that I'd heard at countless weddings: "Love is patient, love is kind. . . . It bears all things, believes all things, hopes all things, endures all things."

That elderly gentleman knew the power of these words. He loved his wife deeply and truly. His feelings for her did not depend on health, strength, or even presence. Although his knees were weak, he was moving forward in a beautiful journey of faithfulness. His wife could not walk with him, but he was carrying love for her in his arms and in his heart.

I turned to gaze at Rachael, who slumbered peacefully in the sun. My other daughter, T.T., couldn't be with us that day, but I could feel that she was present, too. These girls continued to be God's greatest blessings on my life. As their mother, I knew that my love for them was true. How did I know? If they were sick, I'd walk miles and carry a teddy bear—one in each arm—for them—even if my knees were weak.

Receive the Mercies

Prayer

Praise God for the people you love truly and who truly love you. Ask God to bless each and every one of them.

Fasting

Fast from rushing through your journey of life. Take a few moments each day to pay attention to the people God has placed on your path. Through them, you may receive the small mercies of new insights and fresh perspectives.

Almsgiving

Give the alms of informal conversation to a stranger, especially one who seems to be limping.

11

Copy-Machine Dance

I sat in my office one morning, fighting back tears. I had been on leave from my job for three months. During that time, I had invested all my energies into grieving the death of my twenty-three-year-old daughter. The minutes and hours of my days had been spent doing nothing but mourning and sleeping. My full-time job had been managing the relentless ache in my heart. I hadn't smiled in weeks.

Now, however, it was time to step back into my professional role. At the Catholic church where I worked, there were classes to teach, programs to plan, and workshops to present. As the clock on my desk clicked to 7:30, I turned on my computer and began to answer the e-mails that had accumulated in my absence, too many to count. I was grateful that most of the staff would not arrive until 8:00. I would be able to work without interruption.

Ellen, our administrative assistant, peeked into my office. Her desk was just outside my door, next to the copy machine. We had worked with one another for several years, and both of us were accustomed to the early-morning shift. "Welcome back," she said.

A petite mom in her midthirties, Ellen was the definition of hip. She worked at the church during the week but moonlighted on Saturday nights as a singer at a local club. As a professional entertainer, she had a style all her own. Her dark hair was short and sassy, highlighted with blond streaks. She ordered most of her clothes from trendy online sites that most of us at the church had never heard of. She could easily pull off wearing short skirts, clunky jewelry, and dress jeans that flared at the ankle. But it was her shoes that elevated her to the highest level of office coolness. Each day she wore a different pair: stacked heels, chic sandals, flowered pumps.

She saw me reaching for a Kleenex. "I don't know what to say," she said. The compassion expressed on her face spoke volumes.

"Mornings are the hardest for me. If I have a short cry, then I'm good to go," I said.

"I'll remember that."

As the mornings passed, Ellen never said much, but just the sight of her face peeking into my doorway was like sunshine. Even though I sniffled quietly at my desk from about 7:30 until 7:45, she never seemed to mind. It was comforting to know that she was just outside my door, running worship aids and bulletins through the copy machine.

Sometimes when I arrived at work, there would be a vase of flowers on my desk, fresh blooms Ellen had salvaged from altar bouquets that had started to wilt. Other times she would leave a funny card or note on my desk. One morning, she came in and looked down at my shoes. That day I was going to clean out a storage room, and I had worn jeans and a pair of scuffed-up tennis shoes. With firmness, she pointed at my feet and said, "Nancy, don't ever, ever wear those shoes again." I could feel the muscles on my face arching into a smile.

Early one morning, I arrived in the office and saw Ellen at her computer, typing a letter. Her head was bobbing to the beat of a song on the CD player. She swayed to and fro in her office chair. "Hey, I put some new shoes on and suddenly everything's fine," she sang loudly.

I recognized the tune. About a year earlier, I'd heard the song on the radio while driving my daughter back to college. Its catchy beat would make anyone tap her feet.

"That would be a great song for one of your gigs," I'd told Ellen months earlier.

Now, as I walked past her desk, she turned up the volume.

"There will be no crying this morning!" she proclaimed. I looked at her curiously. I wasn't sure I was ready to break my routine of sadness. My daughter was gone and I had developed a nonnegotiable schedule of mourning her loss. If I shed a few measured tears in the morning, I could be productive for most of the workday. What would happen if I disrupted that routine?

Ellen sprang up out of her chair. She was her usual stylish self: pencil-legged jeans, silk blouse, and patent-leather heels. She began to dance. She twirled, snapped her fingers, and belted out the lyrics.

She looked at me. "C'mon, Nancy. It's a church dance-a-thon!" That made me giggle.

"Hey, put on some new shoes! Feel yourself smile." She had me swaying now. In another moment, I was up and dancing, too.

I'm sure we looked ridiculous—singing, swooping, and swirling by the copy machine. But as we danced, I felt something returning. That almost-forgotten joy began to bubble up. Then I heard something I barely recognized: my own laugh.

Almost four years have passed since that morning. Although I have moved on to another job, I will always cherish the memory of that dance. I wish I could say that the joy I felt that morning caused my grief to magically disappear forever. But like all bereaved parents, I know that I will silently mourn my daughter's loss for a lifetime. Still, Ellen gave me a great gift that day. She invited me to take a much-needed break from heartache.

Grief had left me emotionally exhausted. For months I had walked in darkness so deep I doubted I would ever smile again. I could barely get myself out of bed in the morning. Just getting dressed and driving to work each day were major accomplishments.

But that morning, Ellen pulled me into the light of hope. She gave me permission to dance even while living in the reality of grief. She helped me forget, for a few moments, that I was in mourning.

I'd like to think that Ellen's invitation to dance was a fore-shadowing of heaven. Perhaps when we arrive at the door of eternity, God will invite us to exchange the scuffed shoes of our sorrow for the new shoes of everlasting joy. As we twirl with those we have loved and lost, God will proclaim, "No crying today!" There will be no tears. No Kleenex. No sniffling. In the light of God's love, a wondrous song of healing will be heard throughout heaven. "I have turned your mourning into dancing."

And what will become of our worn-out shoes of grief? We will never wear them again.

Receive the Mercies

Prayer

When grief robs you of joy, pray that God will send you a dance partner.

Fasting

In times of sorrow, take a few moments each day to fast from your grief. Receive the small mercy of a hug or an understanding smile. Give yourself permission to take a break from mourning.

Almsgiving

Give the alms of your outstretched hand to a despairing friend. Lead your friend in a dance of hope.

12

The Best Gift

Ike came into my office with his dad at about 5:00 p.m., just as I was making last-minute preparations for my first night of classes. "Well, hello there," I said, looking up from my computer.

That night, Ike's dad was working in the kitchen. In just a couple of hours, the church would be filled to capacity with parents, teenagers, and young children. There would be a dinner in the main hall, a worship service in the church, and then a variety of programs for the children.

"Ike's a hard worker—he can help with just about anything," his father said.

I smiled.

Ike was a redheaded ten-year-old. A shy boy, he barely made eye contact with me. With hands in his pockets, he looked down at the floor.

"Sure," I said. "You can help me count up the Bibles. I'll need about twenty-two of them."

For the next half hour, I put him to work sorting paper clips, rearranging craft supplies, and sharpening pencils. I didn't really need the help, but my intuition told me that Ike needed companionship. He seemed sad.

The next day, I learned that Ike's mother had died from cancer about a year earlier. A coworker told me that his mom had been very active in the church. "She was a selfless person. It's been hard on Ike and his dad."

I wondered how I could reach out to him. Maybe, with time, he would be ready to talk about it.

Over the following few months, I kept my office door wide open, especially on Wednesday nights. That's when Ike showed up, always at five. He never said much, but as the weeks passed, he was always willing to lend a helping hand. "You're my new assistant," I told him.

Sometimes the two of us set up tables in the classrooms. Other times we stapled worksheets or put together bulletin boards in the hallway. One November evening, just before Thanksgiving, I told him, "Let's forget about working tonight—how 'bout if we just eat dinner?"

"That's sounds good," said Ike as we headed to the church kitchen. Minutes later, while we ate tacos and brownies in my office, he said, "My mom died last year."

I nodded my head knowingly. "I bet you miss her."

"Yep, I do." Then he turned his gaze toward the family photographs that were displayed on a shelf above my desk. "Who's that?" He pointed to a picture of a girl grinning widely, her slanted eyes lit up from the inside.

"That's Sarah. She died right about the same time as your mother," I said.

"How old was she?"

"Twenty-three." I put my plate of food down on the desk, feeling as if I needed to clean out the top drawer or sort more papers—anything but talk about this.

"Could she talk?" Ike asked.

"Oh, yes." I grabbed a Kleenex and pretended that I was going to sneeze.

"What was her favorite thing to say?"

As a professional, I was trying so hard to separate my private sorrow from the leadership role I held at the church. But I was a mother, too, even as I sat in this office in a place where I carried out religious work. How could I not feel something for this boy who had just lost his mother? As a parent, I wanted to shield him from hurt and protect him from a sorrow that I could barely comprehend myself.

"'Always follow your heart.' She said that all the time," I said, dabbing at my eyes.

For a few minutes, Ike and I sat in a comfortable silence. As we crunched on our tacos, families passed by the office and waved to us. We waved back.

A few weeks later, Ike played the part of the angel Gabriel in our annual Christmas pageant. On the night of the program, Ike stood on the church stage wearing a white robe and a strand of garland on his head. "Do not be afraid, Mary, for you have found favor with God," he proclaimed to a little girl who was playing the part of Mary. From the back of the church, I watched him while preparing the other children for their parts. Ike's voice was strong and confident. With the lights from the ceiling shining down on him, he looked like how I imagined a real angel would look. "He's the perfect person to play that part," I murmured to those standing close by. Everyone applauded for him at the end of the show.

After the presentation, parents gathered in a large hall with their costumed children. Ike ate cookies while his beaming father received compliments from other parishioners praising his son's performance. "Ike did a fantastic job—he was the star of the show!"

I drew near to Ike and handed him a Christmas card. "Your mom is so proud of you."

"Yep," he said with a wide grin. He looked like such a little man.

"I'm proud of you, too!" I added.

On the morning of Christmas Eve, I tidied up my office before beginning the long holiday break. As the choir practiced in a classroom across the hall, Ike showed up at my office door. He was holding a large gift bag. "Merry Christmas!"

I reached into the bag. Peeling away layers of tissue paper, I found a stuffed bear made out of denim. It had buttons for eyes and a pink bow wrapped around its shoulders.

"It's made from my mom's favorite shirt," Ike said.

I was at a loss for words. I hugged the bear tightly and closed my eyes and imagined the mother who had raised this extraordinary boy.

"Can I put the bear on my shelf?" I asked him.

"That would be OK." He helped me clear a spot for the stuffed bear right next to Sarah's picture.

"This is one of the nicest gifts I have ever received," I said.

Four years later, that bear is still sitting on the same shelf, right above my desk. Ike is about a foot taller than me, an active teenager involved in the youth programs at our church.

He's also a teacher in the children's program on Sunday mornings. He still never says a whole lot, but he doesn't need to. His kindness and compassion speak volumes.

"The younger kids look up to you," I always tell him. I will never forget the Wednesday night he first showed up at my office. We were two broken souls, stranded on the roadside of grief. But there, for a little while, we kept each other company.

We can all keep each other company, especially in times of loss. It isn't all that hard to do. Sometimes it means stapling papers or sorting paper clips or eating tacos with someone who is hurting. Other times it's about sitting in silence with a friend. But most of the time it's simply about sharing the compassion of Christ. That's one of the nicest gifts anyone can receive.

Receive the Mercies

Prayer

Pray that God will give you the gift of compassion. It's a small mercy that will heal many lives.

Fasting

Fast from hiding your heartaches. Let others share them.

Almsgiving

Give the alms of your company to those who are stranded on the road of grief.

Christ has no body now but yours,
No hands, no feet on earth but yours,
Yours are the eyes through which he looks
Compassion on this world
Christ has no body now on earth but yours.

—St. Teresa of Ávila

13

A Holy Interruption

I like that Rachael, my youngest daughter, attends a college just twenty-five minutes from our home. At nineteen years of age, she has her independence, but she still gets home quite often to do her laundry or just to hang out with the family.

On a recent afternoon, as she studied for a test at the kitchen table, I sat across from her, writing on my laptop. While I pecked out paragraphs for an article, Rachael buried her head in a textbook: *Human Anatomy*. She was preparing for a career in the medical profession—perhaps occupational therapy or exercise science. She'd mentioned the desire to work with children who have disabilities.

That afternoon, she studied for an exam by memorizing a long list of anatomical terms. "Buccinator: it's the muscle that makes the lips whistle," she said. I tried to concentrate on my project, but she kept slurping coffee from a ceramic mug. "Zygomaticus: the smiling muscle." From the corner of my eye, I watched her mimic a grin. She memorized the name of every facial muscle, repeating each term out loud.

I was distracted. *This article needs to be done by Monday.* I corrected three typing mistakes and noticed Rachael furrowing her brow. "Frontalis: it wrinkles the forehead."

"Are you hungry for lunch?" I asked, turning off my computer.

"Thanks, Mom."

While I stood at the counter making turkey sandwiches, Rachael turned to another page in her book. "Mom, come here and look at this." I set our lunches on the table and looked at a sketch of a human skull.

"This is amazing—the bones of the skull are joined by sutures. It's like God sewed us together," she said.

"You're right," I replied, adjusting my glasses. Sure enough, the thin connective tissues that held together the bones of the skull had the appearance of thread.

"Mom, it looks just like stitches."

"It does," I said softly.

Soon the words from Psalm 139:13–15 whispered to me: "For it was you who formed my inward parts; you knit me together in my mother's womb. I praise you, for I am fearfully and wonderfully made. Wonderful are your works; that I know very well. My frame was not hidden from you, when I was being made in secret, intricately woven in the depths of the earth."

As we ate our lunch, she continued to study, but I found myself thinking back to when I was pregnant with Rachael, carrying her in my womb. God had fashioned every part of her perfectly, a myriad of tiny muscles, tendons, and tissues that enabled her to smile, whistle, and wrinkle her brow. Before I even saw her, her little bones were being stitched together, the threads of God's love fastening her humanness to heaven.

Rachael belonged to her Creator, not to me. Years earlier, in a sanctuary right beneath my heart, God had breathed life into her. For a little while I had enjoyed the privilege of mothering her. Throughout her childhood I had been her teacher, protector, and guide. In the little kingdom of our family, I had held her hand tightly in mine.

But Rachael had always been on loan to me. Now that she was older, it was clear that God had a calling on her life, one that was beckoning her to serve in a kingdom much vaster than that of our family. From the very beginning, she had been ordained for the work of God. And from the moment I first held her in my arms, I had been ordained to let go.

Rachael took one last bite of her sandwich and handed me her textbook. "Will you help me memorize the neck muscles?" She was completely unaware of the emotions these moments had stirred up in me. "You can read the names of the muscles, and I'll tell you what their function is."

"Deltoid," I said, lifting one arm in the air to wave at her.

Rachael laughed. "It's the muscle that raises the arm."

I could work on my article later. This was a holy interruption, a sacred moment in which to recall my daughter's beginnings and to praise God for the person she was becoming—a woman who understood, on a deep and profound level, the miraculous power of grace.

Today, if someone distracts you, be sure to stop, look, and listen. God may have something to say.

Receive the Mercies

Prayer

Ask God to help you to recognize the holy interruptions in your life.

Fasting

Fast from the need to control each minute of your day. Be open to the small mercies of unexpected conversations. The Lord can speak through anyone.

Almsgiving

Give the alms of your time to someone who longs for it. Your time, given in love, is one of life's most valuable commodities.

14

Grace in the Grocery Store

Sometimes, God's grace is revealed in small ways. For example, one Friday afternoon I went to the grocery store. In my head I carried a list that two of my daughters had given me. That weekend, they were coming home from their busy lives at college and work. "We're bringing friends. Can you pick up some treats? Can we make chocolate-chip cookies?"

I filled my basket with crackers, cheese, and chocolate chips, then strolled down the hair-product aisle. ("We need some shampoo, too.")

As I browsed for their favorite brand, an herbal something or other, I noticed an older woman standing right next to me. Judging from the deep wrinkles in her face and the way she stood hunched over in her floral print shirt, I guessed she was around eighty-five years old. Her graying hair was tied up in a scarf and in her hand were several coupons.

"There's none left," she said, pointing to a sign taped to the edge of an empty shelf. It read: "We are temporarily out of White Rain shampoo. Please see the clerks at the check-out lanes."

I could tell she was disappointed. "That's a bummer," I said.

She gave a little laugh. "It's my favorite shampoo. Have you ever heard of White Rain? It's been around forever."

"I have—my grandmother swore by it."

Mema, my grandmother, had passed away years before. Now I found myself remembering the way her brown eyes used to twinkle beneath her thick bifocals. I remembered, too, the glow that always seemed to radiate from her face.

"It's the best shampoo I've ever bought. It makes your hair shine," the woman said.

Suddenly I was a child again, sitting at Mema's kitchen table on Sunday morning with my family. I could almost smell the cinnamon rolls fresh from her oven and the aroma of coffee percolating in a lime-green pot. I saw her trimming rosebushes in her backyard and remembered the fragrance of rose petals falling from her shears onto the grass.

But the strongest memory was of her linen closet. I could see the neatly folded towels, jars of potpourri, and bottles of White Rain shampoo.

"Do you want a coupon for White Rain? I have an extra one," the woman offered.

"Why, yes, that would be wonderful." My eyes were beginning to mist.

She went on her way, and I lingered in the shampoo aisle, just looking at my coupon for White Rain. That woman didn't know it, but she had blessed my day in a profound way; she had helped me remember my grandmother.

Later, when I unpacked my groceries, I opened the bag of chocolate chips before putting it on the pantry shelf. The aroma of chocolate evoked images from the days when I would make chocolate-chip cookies with my three small children. I could still see them gathered around our kitchen table, their little hands and faces coated with flour and brown sugar: "Mommy, can I crack the eggs?" "Let me stir." "Can we each have two when they're done?"

Just then I looked out the window and saw my two grown daughters pull into the driveway. I watched them and their friends tumble out of the car and imagined them on a future day making chocolate-chip cookies with their own children. Would the smell of chocolate trigger remembrances of the special times we had known? Would their memories bless them? Maybe someday they would understand—as I have today—that the most memorable things in life are little: fragrances of roses, cinnamon, or chocolate; twinkles in aging eyes and smudges on tiny fingers; coupons, little bottles of shampoo.

Receive the Mercies

Prayer

Pray that you might begin to recognize and cherish the small moments that make life so wonderful.

Fasting

Fast from the belief that your little life has no significance. Use your days on earth to bring joy to others.

Almsgiving

Share the alms of your memories with loved ones. Shared remembrances are small mercies that last forever.

15

Mountains

Just a few weeks before my daughter passed away, something beautiful happened. That January night, I was sitting on the couch in our family room watching the nightly news. As I listened to the weather forecast for "another four inches of snow," Sarah drew near and settled in next to me.

Sarah was twenty-three years old but still a young girl in so many ways. Wearing a pink-flannel nightgown trimmed with ruffles, the light in her eyes reminded me of sunshine.

Sarah's two younger sisters were grown up, one in her late teens and the other away at college, but Sarah had remained home with me. I had grown used to the steadiness of her quiet presence and the predictability of her happy countenance.

For a moment, we just smiled at each other. Eighteen months earlier, the doctors had diagnosed her with pulmonary hypertension and told us, "The pressure in her lungs cannot sustain life much longer."

Ever since then, I had convinced myself that Sarah's healing depended on my faith. As a Catholic, I had grown up believing that if I followed a formula of fervent prayer, made regular trips to Mass, and performed a checklist of good deeds, Surely God would answer the pleas of my heart.

I had done everything a committed believer would do. I had taken Sarah to healing services. I had asked friends and family to pray for a miracle. Each day I repeated the same Bible verse: "For truly I tell you, if you have faith the size of a mustard seed, you will say to this mountain, 'Move from here to there,' and it will move; and nothing will be impossible for you" (Matthew 17:20).

But it was becoming clear that my faith wasn't going to move mountains. As the months passed, Sarah ate less and slept more. She was growing weaker by the day, and I felt myself losing control. As her mother, my basic instinct was to protect her from harm. But I was powerless to help her. Many nights I tossed and turned in my bed, angrily fighting it out with God: "How can you turn away from my prayer? Why are you allowing this to happen?"

Yet that night, as Sarah sat next to me, an unexplainable calmness came over me. A voice within seemed to say, "Remember this moment."

I began memorizing the way Sarah looked, the happy glow of her freckled face, the radiance of her dimpled grin, the way her chestnut-brown hair caught the light of a nearby lamp. A mother-daughter love flickered between us like a candle that could never be snuffed out.

She wrapped her hand around mine, clasping it tightly. "You've been a . . . a . . . good mom," she stuttered softly. Her words warmed me even as winter winds blew beyond the window.

Sarah was saying good-bye. She was beckoning me to cherish the past—all the small cumulative moments we had experienced on our journey together. A hundred memories flashed before me. I remembered the small things she had taught me to treasure: dandelions, peanut-butter bars, Starbucks, pink fingernail polish, fairy tales at bedtime, love songs, kitchen-table chats, opening Christmas presents, holding hands, and dancing together in the living room.

"You've been a good daughter," I said, brushing my hand over her hair. I didn't want to miss this opportunity to tell her what an honor it had been to be her mom. She just grinned as if she already knew.

As the newscast ended, Sarah laid her head on my shoulders and began falling asleep. For the first time in months, I felt all the muscles in my neck relax. It had been such a long time since I had rested.

It was the strangest moment. I still felt fearful. My anger at God lingered. These were very natural and necessary feelings, and I could not deny their presence. But in that moment, I no longer felt a need to pray for Sarah's physical healing.

Instead, a much different prayer rose up in me like a mighty peak ascending from a dark valley. "Lord, you've been a good father. I trust you with Sarah's life. Thy will be done."

It was just a small mustard seed of prayer, but it moved the biggest mountain of all: my fear of trusting God completely.

Almost four years have passed since Sarah's death. It's been a difficult journey. Like most bereaved parents, I will never "get over" her loss; but with God's help and the support of loved ones, I have been able to rise from the dark tomb of grief.

I miss her terribly, and not one day goes by that I don't think of her. But now, I often find myself praying in gratitude for the gift of her life. I am especially appreciative of the time we spent together in our family room on that cold January evening. God gave us time to say good-bye to each other. In that sacred farewell came a new understanding of faith.

Although grabbing hold of Bible verses and praying for miracles are wonderful ways to express our faith, we can never predict how the Lord will respond. I'm learning that God is an awesome mystery, beautiful and incomprehensible. Sometimes he answers our prayers in mighty ways. Other times, he settles in next to us as the snow of our suffering begins to fall.

God cherishes our past and will always give us courage to face the future, whatever it might hold. In his presence, we can stop pounding on the doors of heaven and quietly entrust all our cares to him.

As we rest in him, mountains will indeed move. We will learn to trust. We will discover the power of true faith. We will come to believe, despite all the whys, that God is good.

Receive the Mercies

Prayer

Spend some time meditating on the ways in which God is calling you to a deeper walk of faith. How is God asking you to trust him?

Fasting

Fast from frenzied demonstrations of faith. Sit quietly. Feel the comfort of God's presence. Receive the small mercy of his rest.

Almsgiving

Give the alms of your trust to God. This is one of the most powerful expressions of faith.

16

Pounding Pillows

There's a beautiful lake about half a mile from my workplace. On warm summer days, I often spend my lunch hour walking around the pathways that line the shore.

A few weeks back, I put on walking shoes and left my air-conditioned office around noon. That day the temperature was in the nineties, so on my way to the lake, I stopped at the grocery store to pick up something to drink.

I hurried through the crowded store, not wanting to waste any time. But when I came to the checkout line, an elderly woman in front of me was unpacking a cart brimming with groceries. The clerk was elderly, too; he scanned each item slowly and carefully.

I looked at my watch. I had only so many minutes for lunch. *Why did I even stop?*

A well-dressed businessman got in line behind me. "This store needs more cashiers," he said angrily. His salad was neatly packaged in a plastic box.

The elderly woman looked up from her cart. "Let me pay for your salad. Then you won't have to wait," she said, her voice soft spoken. She reached out her hand to him.

The man tightened his grip on his lunch. "No, I've got it," he said gruffly.

"But I'm just being kind. I want to help."

"I'm fine!"

I stood between the two of them, clutching my mineral water. Tension was building. I wondered who would give in first.

"Well, I certainly can't help you if you don't want to be helped!" she told him.

"I don't believe this." The man threw his boxed salad at a magazine rack and walked out of the grocery store.

A few minutes later, I found myself strolling along the peaceful lakeside. As I passed a fragrant rose garden, I started thinking about the businessman. What had made him so angry? Was it his ego? Was it embarrassing for him to let an aged woman pay for his salad? Why was he so unable to receive her offer of help? I decided that he probably had a lot of pent-up anger.

I picked up my stride and remembered how angry I'd become after my daughter's death. I had tried to convince myself that my relationship with God was intact. In my daily devotions, I praised God for being light in my darkness. As I slept through the awfulness of grief, I sought the Lord's comfort and asked for his strength. While facing the constant presence of my child's absence, I lit candles and stared at the flames.

It was much easier to endure my feelings of sorrow than to admit that I was enraged at the Creator of the universe. But sometimes my jaw felt so tight that I could hardly talk. Other times I felt like taking a baseball bat and smashing it against the trees in our backyard. Often, my other two daughters watched me as I slammed the mop over our kitchen floor and jammed it into corners. "Mom, what's wrong?"

Everyone but me seemed to recognize that I was furious.

One afternoon, my sister Peggy sat at my kitchen table and said, "There are so many people who want to help you, but you have to let them."

"I'm fine."

Then, one afternoon, I went out to breakfast with Ruth, a close friend. As we ate our eggs and toast, she handed me a gift bag filled with three throw pillows. "These are for pounding."

"Pounding?"

"Every time you feel mad at God, pound the heck out of them."

A few days later, I found myself home alone. The girls had gone out to an afternoon football game. Carrying the bag of pillows, I made my way down the stairs that led to our basement.

I lined the pillows up on an old couch that we rarely used, spacing them evenly. For a moment, I just stared at them. I could feel all the muscles in my jaw tightening. "It's not fair," I said softly. I closed my eyes and tightened both hands into fists. I imagined that God was standing in the room. "It's not fair," I said, much louder than before.

I picked up one of the pillows and threw it against the wall. "No parent should have to bury a child!" I kicked another pillow across the floor. I kept kicking it. "I'm tired of grief! I'm tired of sleeping and crying and hurting!" I pounded the third pillow with my clenched fist, again and again and again. "Why did you let this happen?" I cried out to God.

I spent a good half hour pounding those throw pillows. It wasn't a pretty sight, a grieving mom suddenly in tune with her rage. But that moment was a turning point in my faith life. I was sharing my secrets with God. I was visiting the dark cellar of my true and nonnegotiable feelings. I was confronting the wrongness, the unfairness, and the utter awfulness of losing my child.

In the days and weeks to come, God and I had regular showdowns in the basement. As I pounded pillows until they were flattened, it didn't seem that I was praying—but I was. God and I were communicating on a deep and personal level. I was sharing confidential information with my truest friend—all the sadness, fear, and anger I had tried so hard to deny. And God listened. That, I discovered, is what I needed most of all.

Four years later, as I walked along a lakeside path, I let myself rest in the wisdom I had gained during those first months of grief. The Lord has given each of us a capacity to feel deeply. We need to react, in some way, to the painful experiences that are part of life. We would not be fully alive if we couldn't cry or kick or shout.

We can always come to God just as we are. Our lives don't need to be perfect. And although we need to find healthy ways to express our anger, God will love us whether our hands are raised in praise or clenched into fists.

Today, if you are struggling with anger, don't pretend it's not there. Make your way down to the cellar of your soul. It might be a dark place, but the light of God's presence waits for you there. Be honest with God. Pound a few pillows. Don't be afraid to shout out your pain.

Rest assured that the King of the universe will hold you close and listen. That might be what you need most of all.

Receive the Mercies

Prayer

Examine your heart. Ask yourself, "What feelings are hardest for me to express to God?"

Fasting

Fast from harboring anger in your heart. Share your resentments with God. Let the small mercy of truth strengthen your relationship with Christ.

Almsgiving

Give the alms of a throw pillow to a hurting friend. Encourage your friend to express anger in a healthy way.

17

Graduation Day

On a sunny afternoon in May, my daughter Christina, who we call T.T., graduated from college. Underneath a powdery blue sky, families and friends of the graduates began gathering for the ceremony in the football stadium lined with folding chairs. The fragrance of blooming lilacs filled the air.

I walked with Rachael, my then-nineteen-year-old daughter. With us was Don, my former spouse. We took our places near an area designated for the graduates.

As we waited for the ceremony to start, my thoughts drifted. Christina and I had met for coffee just a week earlier. As often happened, we ended up reminiscing about the family member who would be absent at the graduation—Sarah. "She was always my best friend," said T.T.

I smiled. Twenty-one years earlier, when we brought home newborn Christina, Sarah had just celebrated her third birthday. "I am the big sister!" she had proclaimed. She cradled baby Christina tenderly for the first time. Almost immediately, the two of them formed a bond.

When Christina grew to toddler stage, she surpassed her sister developmentally. Blessed with the gifts of natural intelligence and intuition, little Christina quickly took on the role of caretaker. She began helping Sarah write her name, comb her hair, zip up a dress, tie her shoes, turn on the television, brush her teeth, make her bed, and put on pretend lipstick.

"You had to grow up so fast," I had said one day. Christina's green eyes misted over.

"Sarah needed me." She recalled a day when we had gone swimming as a family at the YMCA when Christina was eight. Sarah kept twirling around and around in the pool, completely unaware that a group of young boys was laughing at her.

"Stop being mean to my sister—she's handicapped!" I could still see Christina standing at the poolside in her little pink bathing suit. Glaring at the boys, I pulled Christina aside and said, "They don't understand."

"I wish that had never happened," I said to her now.

I could see that she was still remembering. "High school was the hardest," she said.

When Christina was in her teens, we sent her to a Catholic high school. She was a straight-A student, and we wanted her to have access to a variety of academic challenges. But we had another, more pressing reason for placing her in a private school. With Sarah attending special education programs near our home, Christina would be away from her and therefore free of the temptation to be her caretaker.

"I told only a few of my high school friends that I had a Down's syndrome sister," she once confided. "I didn't want to risk being teased."

"I'm so sorry," I said. I wanted to rewrite time. I wanted to go back and rescue her from all the prejudice and insensitivity she had experienced as Sarah's sister.

The stadium began to swell with people, a sea of parents in suits and sundresses. Rachael checked her digital camera. A soft wind blew while Don and I reminisced about Christina's growing up.

I looked toward the campus that overlooked the stadium. For the past four years, this had been Christina's home away from home, a little city of Gothic-style buildings trimmed with steeples and stained glass that glistened among grass-covered hills.

The familiar sound of "Pomp and Circumstance" began playing as the faculty, donned in regal caps, gowns, and sashes, assembled on the stage. Soon a long line of graduates began processing down a curvy sidewalk toward the stadium, their black caps and gowns shimmering against a hedge of purple lilac bushes.

Cameras snapped. Parents and grandparents sniffled. As the graduates were seated, parents strained their necks, hoping to catch a glance of their son or daughter.

In the midst of it all, a profound image appeared in my mind's eye: a Sunday in January, a few weeks before Sarah died. As I passed our family room, I saw Sarah and Christina sitting on the couch. As on most Sunday afternoons, the two of them were watching reruns of *Full House*. They snuggled together in a quilt, holding hands, their heads touching. "You're my best friend," I heard Christina tell her sister. "You are my best friend, too," said Sarah.

A distinguished speaker—a congressman from Minnesota—addressed the graduates. "You are the light of the world. A city that is set on a hill cannot be hidden." He was quoting the familiar passage from the fifth chapter of Matthew's Gospel. The speaker encouraged the graduates to go out and shine their lights.

It was clear to me that God had prepared Christina for this important moment. Throughout her young life, God had been at work, laying a foundation for her to work with the poor and disabled. Although her college education had taught her the how-tos of social work, it was Sarah who had tutored her in the ways of compassion, courage, and unconditional love.

Then the names of the graduates were read, and they ascended the stage, one by one, to receive their diplomas. After Christina left the stage, she passed our row, smiling and waving her diploma. Underneath her cap, her long dark hair blew in the wind. We waved wildly. "Way to go!" Don called out. I could only blow her a kiss. I closed my eyes and listened to cameras snapping and families cheering. I knew that Sarah was rejoicing with us.

And Christina was ready to shine her light.

Receive the Mercies

Prayer

Take a moment to thank God for the people who have influenced your life choices. Rejoice in the ways they have prepared you to live out your divine calling.

Fasting

Fast from hiding your light. With great humility, share your gifts with those who are weak, poor, or otherwise disadvantaged in this world. Teach them; but more important, let them teach you.

Almsgiving

Give the alms of your applause to a young person. Cheer them on as they pursue their dreams.

18

My Mother's Garden

It was a warm morning in June, my mother's eighty-first birthday. "My gift to you is working in your garden," I had told her. Now as I knelt in the dirt by her deck, I pulled weeds and began loosening the soil with a small shovel. I felt ready for a day of gardening.

"Where do you want the marigolds?" I asked Mom. She was sitting close by on a lawn chair. Her thick glasses reflected the sunlight, and her short silvery hair had just been styled at the beauty shop. She was still a very classy-looking lady. Wearing a floral top and yellow capris, she turned the pages of a book titled *The Flower Doctor*. "Anywhere is fine," she answered.

Underneath a cloudless sky, I began spacing a variety of flowers we had just bought at the grocery store: petunias, geraniums, and impatiens. "It says here that impatiens like the shade," she said as she turned to the index of her book. I pretended that I didn't know this well-known flower fact. "Oh, really?"

A warm breeze blew through the yard, and I starting thinking back on the years gone by.

When I was in high school, my mom and I fought constantly. I could remember her nagging: "You wear too much makeup; your room looks like a cyclone struck it; your handwriting is atrocious."

One night, when I was about seventeen, we argued about a boy I was dating. "He's too old for you!" I had rushed out of our house, slamming the front door loudly. "You are the worst mother!"

The fights continued through my college years. One autumn afternoon, when I was a sophomore, my parents came to visit me at my off-campus house. At the time I was living in a run-down home with three roommates, one of them a male friend who wore bib overalls and smoked cigarettes.

I was just happy to be on my own—no matter that the roof of our house leaked and there was no working stove. While my dad checked the basement for rodents, my mom walked into the kitchen, where I was cooking a can of peas in a Crock-Pot. All she said was, "This is ridiculous!" Standing there in a tie-dyed shirt, I rolled my eyes and stirred the peas.

The biggest fight of all happened when I was in my midthirties and started writing for national publications. In one of my articles, published in *Reader's Digest*, I made mention that someone in my family had struggled with alcoholism. After reading the article, my mother called me and sobbed so loudly that I had to hold the phone away from my ear. "I can't believe you wrote that!"

I honestly didn't know what to say. It was just one sentence, tucked away in a story that highlighted the power of friendship and hope. "I didn't mean to hurt you." She was inconsolable. She didn't speak to me for months. I tried writing her letters of apology. I often called her, but she never answered the phone. I ended many days with the prayer that we would be reconciled.

Then, one afternoon while I was signing books at a bookstore, she showed up. At first she hovered near a display, paging through magazines. When the store was about to close, she slowly drew near to my table. "About the article . . ." Her lower lip began to quiver.

I took a deep breath. "Mom, I'm so sorry."

She reached out and hugged me tightly. "I know the story was true, but did you have to tell twenty-seven million people?" I could feel her shoulders shaking. "I love you," she said. I patted her on the back. "I love you, too."

The bookstore memory faded. As I began to plant zinnias, I noticed how warm the sun felt on my shoulders. "I can't wait until everything is in full bloom," Mom said from her chair.

Now, nearly twenty years past that big rift between us, I had a whole new appreciation for my mother. Although she was strong willed and highly sensitive, those qualities had served her well. Her life had not been easy. She had grown up during the Great Depression, had lived in a home without a bathroom, and had used orange crates for furniture. When she was just nine years old, her older brother Bud was killed in World War II. During the years she spent raising me and my nine other siblings, she worked tirelessly, even taking on a part-time job at a hardware store to help my dad make ends meet. While growing up, I had watched the way my mom always took charge of her life. Even after Dad died at the age of fifty-six, Mom went on to find a full-time job as a secretary. She redecorated her home. She made new friends. I don't ever remember her complaining about how difficult her life had been.

"Where do you want the rosebush?" I asked. I had bought her a climbing rose vine for her birthday. "Hmm . . . Let's put it by the fence. I'll be able to see it from the kitchen window."

I dug a hole near the fence and tucked the base of the rosebush into it. As I patted the soil around it, I realized that my mother and I were more alike than we were different. Our lives had been intertwined for decades, like two colored ribbons, braided together.

I, too, had become single after many years of marriage. In the months that followed my divorce, my mother never said much about the changes that had come to my life. Instead, she invited me to go to estate sales with her on Saturday mornings. As we scoured through homes filled with bargain-priced furniture and used appliances, she would secretly purchase a new tablecloth for my kitchen or a trinket for my bathroom. "It will be good for you to redecorate your house," she would say. "That will help you move on."

Then, after Sarah died, I would often lie on the couch in my mother's living room, unable to do much of anything. "I don't think I can go on," I told her one afternoon.

"You have to go on. You have two other children and a lot of life ahead."

That made me angry. *What does she know about losing a child?* But that afternoon, she sat down beside me and began sharing stories about her brother Bud. "Before he went off to war, he made me a crib for my doll. It was the most precious gift I have ever received." Her grief, though decades old, seemed as fresh as mine. She was trying to comfort me.

She was trying to say, "I understand, in some small way, how much you miss your child."

The fragrance of freshly planted roses drifted through the air. After a day of digging and planting, my mother's weed-filled garden was finally transformed into a visual feast of color. I watered the last geranium and flopped down on the grass next to her lawn chair.

That morning, I had come to this garden ready to shovel and till the dirt. But here, in Mom's backyard, I had unearthed much more than soil. On my mom's eighty-first birthday, the treasure of our shared history had been uncovered. I now understood what a gift her life had been to me.

"Look, Mom." I pointed as a little bird with orange wings rested on her rosebush.

"Oh, my." She adjusted her glasses. Her face was aglow. We linked arms and watched as the bird sang its own little tune.

We had weathered some difficult times as mother and daughter, but we were bonded by mutual love and respect. Together we had pulled the weeds of resentment from our relationship. We had buried all our bitterness in the ground of forgiveness. We had watched each other bloom from unexpected loss to resurrection and new life.

Receive the Mercies

Prayer

Give thanks to God for those who have guided you.

Fasting

Fast from harboring bitterness. Let the small mercy of unconditional acceptance free you.

Almsgiving

Give the alms of forgiveness freely.

19

Another Great Day of Life

Some mercies are not small at all—they are huge and life changing. One such mercy for me is a lesson I learned over the span of my daughter's life. Sarah taught me, over and over, that every day is a gift.

She began imparting this truth during her first months, cold winter weeks filled with trips to the hospital and long stays in intensive care. Day after day, she lay in her stainless-steel crib, surrounded by doctors, IV machines, and beeping monitors. Yet in the midst of so much uncertainty, she slept peacefully. As I look back on those days, it seems that she was saying, "These days are sacred. I'm being healed right before your eyes."

And she *was* healed. After her first year, she was free from most of the health constraints that defined her early infancy. She never went through her terrible twos, threes, or fours. She was too busy defying her disability, grinning widely as she slowly learned to walk, talk, sing, paint, and draw. "Mom, I m-m-made this just for you," she would stutter as each day I hung one of her new paintings on the fridge.

I've saved most of her early artwork. My favorite is a picture of a flower with petals of hearts. It reminds me that God's love can be found in unexpected places.

Love was very important to Sarah. Her childhood years created a quiet song of kindness and compassion, one she would teach all of us to sing. When she was given a candy bar, she would share the greater portion. When her two younger sisters argued over a toy, she would step between them and say, "Be nice!" On days when I was overwhelmed with the nonstop demands of motherhood, she would pat me on the back and say, "It . . . it will b-be OK."

Maybe her love for love was why she developed a fondness for fairy tales. As a little girl, she was fascinated with Cinderella, Snow White, Belle from *Beauty and the Beast*, and all the other make-believe maidens who were transformed by the power of love.

I can still see myself as a young mother, cuddling with Sarah and her sisters on the couch in our family room. While paging through stories of kings and castles, Sarah sat on my lap with a silver tiara on her head. Every afternoon, as I read the timeworn tales, she would glide her tiny fingers over each word. Sometimes she would lean into the pages and her pink-framed glasses would slide right off her nose.

One day, as we read Snow White, she pointed to a picture of a crowned princess dressed in a powder-blue gown. "Mom . . . that's . . . that's me!" She jumped up and danced around the family room like a little ballerina. "I'm . . . I'm . . . loved," she proclaimed.

Sarah's unwavering joy brought comfort to me, especially on days when I couldn't help but worry about her future. I was never sure if it was her disability or her innate goodness that rendered her incapable of thinking unkind thoughts or speaking hurtful words. She didn't understand sin. She was perplexed by bitterness, resentment, and unforgiveness. "Sarah, you have a pure heart," I told her often. "I know," she would say, eyes shimmering.

As she moved into her teenage years, Sarah became more pensive and began penning her thoughts on the inside covers of her fairy-tale books. Each afternoon, when she arrived home from her special education program, she would sit at her desk, beneath a shelf that held her collection of crowns. Dressed in one of my old bridesmaid gowns, She would open her books and begin crafting her messages: "My name is Prncess Sarah . . . I alwys fllow my dreams . . . I hav a perfct life."

Sometimes as I passed by her room with a laundry basket in my arms, I would take a peek at her work. "Mom, I . . . I'm . . . writing about all . . . all the g-good things in life," she would say.

She never once lamented about what she couldn't do. Instead, she read love stories. She drew inspiring pictures. She wrote beautiful messages. She dressed up on ordinary afternoons. She danced. She smiled. She treasured each day of her life.

Were there days when her disability was hard on me? Did I have moments when I wished that everything were different? Was I ever angry at God? Of course.

But now that Sarah is safe in God's arms, I can't seem to recall the hard days. Maybe that's because her life is now a montage of memories, all about love.

Each morning, as the clock in the hallway chimed five, Sarah tiptoed into my room and stood by my bedside. Dressed in flowered pajamas, she would nudge me gently and whisper, "Mom, wake up! It's . . . it's another great day of l-life."

These days, when I wake up in the morning, I let Sarah's words speak to me anew. Even on bad days, when I would rather stay curled up in bed, grieving my losses, I hear her admonition to get up and start living my life. As I rise, I hold her memory close to me—like a flower petaled with hearts.

Yes, life is a gift. And each day it waits to be opened.

Receive the Mercies

Prayer
Pray that God will help you cherish each of your days on earth, even the hardest ones.

Fasting
Fast from lamenting over the things you can't do. Start using your gifts and talents to further God's kingdom on earth. Be a person who shares the small mercies of kindness, compassion, and love.

Almsgiving
Give the alms of your presence to a person who is disabled or disadvantaged in some way. Be prepared to receive more than you give.

20

Yahoo!

A thunderstorm had kept me up the night before. Now, as the morning sunlight broke through the clouds, the rain-coated grass sparkled. Although a few raindrops were still falling, I sat down on a park bench.

It was a Sunday morning in September. The trees were just beginning to change color. All the houses that framed the park were quiet and still. As the bells from a nearby church chimed out seven o'clock, it seemed that my entire hometown was still slumbering.

I leaned back on the bench. "It's finally done," I said. I had been up most of the night finishing the manuscript for the *Small Mercies* book. While lightning had flashed outside my kitchen window, I sat at my computer typing out the last story. In a few days, I would send it off to the publisher.

In the distance, I could hear a train rolling across a riverside track. I wondered what the front cover of my book might look like. And I imagined you, the reader. I envisioned you curled up in a chair holding a Kindle or turning the pages of a book. Would the stories I have written speak to you? Had you known similar joys and struggles?

As I thought about you, I couldn't help but feel vulnerable. For such a long time, I had been the keeper of these stories. I had lived them, felt them, and processed them in the privacy of my soul. I had spent hours writing them alone at my kitchen table. Now I was releasing these reflections, which soar from my life to yours.

Would you, the reader, think that I was just a grieving mother trying to process the devastating loss of her child? I imagined the readers who might be uncomfortable that I am a divorced Catholic. Because I had taken the risk of inscribing my secret fears and failings, surely some readers would think, *What a mess her life has been!*

As I thought about all these things, I saw a boy with Down's syndrome riding his bike on a sidewalk near the playground. He gripped the high handlebars, a perpetual smile on his face. I didn't know his name but had seen him from time to time, riding around the park. On many occasions, I had tried to greet him as he steered past. "Hi there!" But he had never once answered back. In fact, he had never as much as made eye contact with me.

But on this morning he steered his bike toward my bench and stopped to rest for a moment. He looked at me, tilting his head as if he were trying to read my thoughts. Lifting his right hand high in the air, he shouted: "Yahooooooooooo!" For several seconds, his mouth was shaped into a perfect *O*.

"Yahoo to you, too." I answered.

With that, he got back on his bike and started pedaling around the park as usual. "Yahooooooooooooo!" he called out again and again. His voice rang through the morning air like the happy praise of angels.

"Yahoo," I whispered to God. Again and again I repeated the word as if it were an alleluia. I closed my eyes and offered this litany to heaven:

Yahoo that God is always with us. Yahoo that life doesn't have to be perfect to be wonderful. Yahoo for family, friendship, and forgiveness. Yahoo for dogs named Sabbath, teddy bears to cuddle, and smoothies we've never tried before. Yahoo for used wicker chairs, statues of Jesus, and twitches of hope. Yahoo that love is stronger than death and that grief cannot, and will not, last forever. Yahoo that resurrection will surely come to all who believe.

I looked up to the sky and watched the clouds give way to a rainbow. As a prism of color arched over the park, a sun shower began to fall. I reached out my hands to catch a few sprinkles. I heard God say, "I'm right here."

My life was a gift—all of it. Through grace, I had found God in every mess, burden, and blessing. God's small mercies had covered me like a rainbow in the clouds.

And *your* life is a gift. Each day is sacred, even the worst one. Every morning, you and I receive an opportunity to experience the presence of Christ in a new way. As the Scriptures tell us: "The steadfast love of the Lord never ceases, his mercies never come to an end; they are new every morning; great is your faithfulness" (Lamentations 3:22).

This means that when we wake up to a new day, we can trust that the Lord will be with us. Although he might reveal himself to us with thunderous signs from heaven, we can usually catch a better glimpse of him in the everyday places and faces that define our lives.

So try looking for God in ordinary places: your home, your workplace, your community. Meet God face-to-face at the grocery store or a coffee shop. Even in the hardest moments, know that you will find God in the compassion of those who love you.

Praise God for your imperfect life.

Shout "Yahoo!" that God remains faithful, despite the challenges you have known.

Stand in the rain of God's love and catch the small mercies that are showering over your life. They're everywhere.

Acknowledgments

I wish to thank all those who brought this book to life.

Joe Durepos: Thanks for rejecting the first two manuscripts that I sent to Loyola. In the end, just the right idea emerged.

Steve Connor: I'm so glad I landed at Loyola. Thanks for giving me the opportunity to write about the hard stuff.

Vinita Wright: Praise you for being one of the best editors I have ever known. You challenged me to visit the cellar of my soul, that place where the deepest truths reside. I needed to go there. Thanks for all the wisdom you have shared.

My big Irish Catholic Family: You have lived and breathed these stories with me. Your names are written on my heart: Jeanne, Rick, Kathy, Mike, Peggy, Tom, Julie, Paul, Johnny, Laurie, Timmy, Mary Beth, Annie, Bill, Terry, Andrea, Lindsey, Josh, Andy, Joe, Kelly, Jenny, Stephen, Kristin,

Christina, Rachael, Patrick, Markie, J.R., Nolan, Rebecca, Ellie and Dillon. Oh Mom . . . I love you dearly.

To my lifelong friends: Thanks for walking with me through my losses. I know it wasn't easy, but you never abandoned me on the journey. Hugs to you: Karen Blomgren, Deb Dooher-Anderson, Sharon Fries, Laurie Belland, Rachael Amundson, Mary Lundsten, and Ruth Ann Ische.